I0893867

EDGE BOOKS

THE GUYS' GUIDE TO MAKING EVERY DAY MORE AWESOME

BY ERIC BRAUN

CAPSTONE PRESS
a capstone imprint

Edge Books are published by Capstone Press,
1710 Roe Crest Drive, North Mankato, Minnesota 56003
www.capstonepub.com

Copyright © 2014 by Capstone Press, a Capstone imprint. All rights reserved. No part of this publication may be reproduced in whole or in part, or stored in a retrieval system, or transmitted in any form or by any means, electronic, mechanical, photocopying, recording, or otherwise, without written permission of the publisher.

Library of Congress Cataloging-in-Publication Data
Braun, Eric, 1971–
The guys' guide to making every day more awesome / by Eric Braun.
pages cm.—(Edge books. the guys' guides)
Includes bibliographical references and index.
Summary: "Describes various tips, activities, and useful information for making every day more fun and productive"—Provided by publisher.
ISBN 978-1-4765-3924-9 (library binding)
ISBN 978-1-4765-5972-8 (ebook pdf)
1. Boys—Life skills guides—Juvenile literature. I. Title.
HQ775.B664 2014
305.230811—dc23 2013035405

Editorial Credits
Aaron Sautter, editor; Veronica Scott, designer; Eric Gohl, media researcher; Jennifer Walker, production specialist

Photo Credits
Capstone Studio: Karon Dubke, 12–13 (background), 13 (bottom), 16 (football toy), 17 (top), 18–19 (all), 26, 27; Corbis: Reuters/Luke MacGregor, 21; Getty Images: PhotoQuest, 7; Newscom: Album/Dreamworks, 17 (bottom), ZUMA Press/Vaughn Youtz, 20; Shutterstock: 1973kla, 2, Aigars Reinholds, 9 (bottom), Aleks Melnik, 11 (ball and mictrophone), Alena Hovorkova, 10 (doodles), Anastasiia Kucherenko, 22 (all), Artex67, 6, Barnaby Chambers, 29 (top left & bottom), BONNINSTUDIO, 25 (top), buttet, 5 (top), Danielbotha, 28 (left), Dariush M, 8 (bottom left), Denis Semenchenko, 25 (bottom), dotshock, 9 (top), Elinalee, 14–15 (background), George Muresan, 5 (bottom), Igor Yanovskiy, cover, Jan Mika, 29 (top right), KUCO, 10 (cello player), Kudryashka, 12–13 (food doodles), makar, 11 (tree), Merggy, 15, Monkey Business Images, 8 (top), Oxygen64, 16–17 (film reel), Pirha, 11 (drawing hand), plastique, 8 (bottom right), Rudy Umans, 28 (right), Suzanne Tucker, 4 (top), Sergey Nivens, 4 (bottom), Vinata, 24–25 (background), zayats-and-zayats, 24, zeber, 28–29 (background)

Design Elements
Shutterstock

Printed in the United States of America in Stevens Point, Wisconsin.
092013 007768WZS14

TABLE OF CONTENTS

SEIZE THE DAY!

When the bell rings at the end of the school day, what do you do? You have no homework and a wide-open afternoon. You could just head home and watch TV. Maybe you could play video games with your friends. Or instead, perhaps you could do something new, challenging, and adventurous!

Every day has opportunities to do awesome things. This book has lots of ideas for making your days more awesome. You'll learn how to make a movie, start your own business, study better for tests, and a lot more. Try the ideas inside or make up your own. Be creative and challenge yourself to make each day as awesome as it can be!

INVENT A SECRET CODE

You and your friend created an awesome battle plan for an upcoming laser tag match. But a guy from the other team saw your notes, and now he knows your strategy! What do you do when you need to keep information secret? You could write it down using a **cipher**. Here's one kind you can try.

1. Write your message in capital letters on two separate lines. Alternate each letter on different lines as shown:

SNEAK ALONG GARDEN FENCE = S E K L N G R E F N E
N A A O G A D N E C

2. If needed, add an extra letter to the bottom line so each line has the same number of letters.

SNEAK ALONG GARDEN FENCE = S E K L N G R E F N E
N A A O G A D N E C X

3. Next, write out the letters in line one and then line two in a single row. Break up the letters into groups to create nonsense words of different lengths.

SEK LNGR EF NENA A OGAD NECX

---

cipher—a code that uses letters or symbols to represent letters of the alphabet

4. To solve the code, your friend will count the letters and divide them in half. Then he puts the first half on top and the second half underneath as you had them before.

SEK LNGR EF NE / NA A OGAD NECX = S E K L N G R E F N E
N A A O G A D N E C X

5. Your friend can then rewrite the secret message by placing alternate letters together to form the words. He'll know to ignore any extra letters at the end.

S E K L N G R E F N E = SNEAK ALONG GARDEN FENCE
N A A O G A D N E C

THE UNBREAKABLE CODE OF THE NAVAJO CODE TALKERS

Early in World War II (1939–1945), the Japanese were easily cracking codes used by the Allies. The United States recruited Navajo Indians to help create better codes. The Navajo language has no alphabet and is very hard to master. The Navajo "code talkers" used Navajo words to describe military terms. For example, the Navajo word *Jay-sho* means "buzzard." In the code, Jay-sho meant "bomber plane." The word for "turtle" meant "tank," and the word for "black sheep" meant "squad." Using this system, the Navajo could communicate complex messages in seconds—and enemies never cracked it.

MAKE SOME MONEY

Want to earn some extra cash? Start your own business! Give your business a cool name and spread the word by making fliers and posters. You could even team up with a friend to make it more fun. Here are a few ideas to get you started.

SELL VEGETABLES AND PLANTS

Order cheap seeds in the fall. Then plant them in pots and grow them indoors during the winter. In the spring you'll have plants to sell for a nice profit.

CHORE SERVICE

Most everyone hates doing household chores. But chores aren't so bad when you're getting paid for them. Many people are willing to pay someone to do their housework for them.

PET-SITTING OR DOG-WALKING

People love their furry friends. They'll often pay an honest and dependable person to take care of their pets when they're away from home.

PLAY IN A BAND

If you and your friends can play instruments, form a band. Learn some songs and put on some shows in the neighborhood. Rock on!

LAWN AND SNOW SERVICE

You can make a lot of extra cash by mowing and raking people's lawns during the summer. During winter you can shovel snow off their driveways and sidewalks.

BE A WRITER AND PUBLISHER

If you like to write stories, you can start a neighborhood magazine or newsletter to sell in your community. Is there an owl or woodpecker that lives in a nearby park? Take a picture and write a short piece for your magazine. Did someone on your block win a prize for the biggest pumpkin? Do an interview and write a story about it. You get the idea. People love to read about cool stuff going on in their area. If your newsletter becomes popular, you can make even more money by selling advertising space like big newspapers and magazines do.

HOW ARE YOU SMART?

Being smart isn't just about doing well on tests and getting good grades. Some scientists believe people have at least eight different kinds of intelligence. Everyone has strengths and weaknesses in the various types of intelligence. Read about them below, and then see if you can recognize yourself in any of them.

1. VERBAL INTELLIGENCE

SMART WITH WORDS. People in this group might like to read, write, or do public speaking.

2. MUSICAL INTELLIGENCE

SMART WITH MUSIC AND SOUNDS. This group is talented at playing instruments and understanding music.

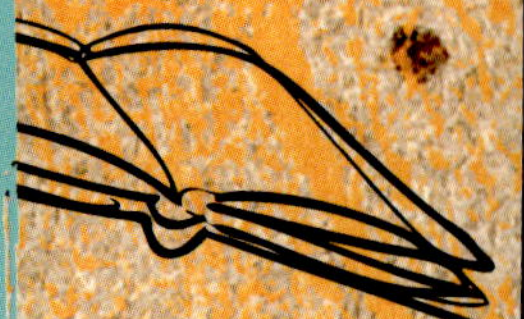

3. MATHEMATICAL INTELLIGENCE

SMART WITH NUMBERS, PATTERNS, AND SCIENCE. These people like mathematical puzzles, riddles, and doing science experiments.

4. VISUAL INTELLIGENCE

SMART WITH IMAGES. People who are visual often have artistic talents and skills such as drawing, painting, and designing things. They also often have a good sense of direction and are good at organizing things in small spaces.

intelligence—the ability to learn and understand information

5. BODY INTELLIGENCE

PHYSICALLY SMART. This group includes people who are good athletes and dancers. These people are also often good at fixing things and working with their hands.

6. INTERPERSONAL INTELLIGENCE

SMART WITH PEOPLE AND SOCIAL SITUATIONS. People strong in this area often find it easy to relate to others. They are often seen as leaders and have lots of friends.

7. INTRAPERSONAL INTELLIGENCE

SMART ABOUT YOURSELF. These people know themselves well. They understand their own strengths and weaknesses. They're also good at thinking about the future and making goals for themselves.

8. NATURALIST INTELLIGENCE

SMART ABOUT NATURE. This group of people feels a strong connection to nature. They might be skilled at studying plants, animals, and the wilderness.

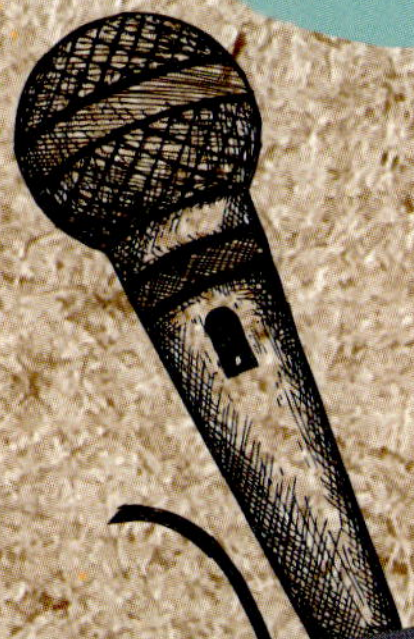

EAT TO GET SMARTER

You probably know that vegetables are better for you than potato chips. But did you know that some foods are great for your brain as well as your body? These foods can help you focus on your work and manage your emotions. Look for foods that are filled with vitamins, protein, and healthy fats and oils.

Here are some great foods to help increase your energy and brainpower. Loading up on these superfoods instead of junk food can help you do better at school and in life.

- **OILY FISH:** Fish such as salmon and tuna are loaded with protein and healthy oils. They help keep your brain healthy so you can stay sharp and focused.
- **SEEDS AND NUTS:** Pistachios, walnuts, pumpkin seeds, sunflower seeds, and other seeds and nuts are loaded with protein and healthy fats. They make great snacks.
- **MILK:** Milk is full of calcium that helps strengthen your bones. It's also a terrific source of vitamins and protein.
- **EGGS:** Eggs are crammed full of vitamins, protein, iron, healthy fats, and more. They're good for your eyes and your brain, help prevent cancer and heart disease, and have several other health benefits.

- **COLORFUL VEGGIES:** Spinach, bell peppers, carrots, tomatoes, broccoli, and beets are all powerful vegetables. The more colorful they are, the more vitamins that are packed into them. Eat a variety of colorful veggies to get all the healthy vitamins your body needs.

Ever get hungry for an after-school snack? Want something to munch on during your next nature hike? Try out this healthy trail mix. It's loaded with good stuff to boost your energy and help you focus on your tasks instead of your stomach.

HEALTHY TRAIL MIX

In a large bowl, mix together ½ cup (120-ml) of each of the following ingredients. After mixing, store in an airtight container for up to one month.

- raisins
- peanuts
- sunflower seeds
- dried fruit (cranberries, cherries, pineapple chunks, or banana chips)
- unsalted nuts (almonds, walnuts, pecans, or cashews)
- mini pretzels
- granola clusters
- chocolate chips, peanut butter chips, or candy-coated chocolates

DO BETTER ON TESTS

Do you dread taking tests at school? Do you stay up late trying to cram every last fact into your brain? Stop worrying. Stressing out about tests won't help. Here are a few ways you can relax and have more confidence while taking tests.

BEFORE THE TEST

Get a good night's sleep: Students need at least 10 hours of sleep a night. If you're sleepy you won't be able to think clearly. Being tired can put you in a bad mood. This can lead to more stress and cause you to perform poorly on your test.

Study: That's a no-brainer, right? But don't wait until the last minute. Studying a little every day for several days is better than cramming everything in at the last minute.

Eat well: The day of the test, eat a healthy breakfast. Being hungry will keep you from thinking clearly and focusing on the test. Eggs are an excellent superfood loaded with brain-boosting protein.

Drink plenty of water: Keep your body and brain **hydrated**. If it's allowed, bring along a bottle of water to your test.

hydrate—to achieve a healthy balance of fluids in the body

DURING THE TEST

Chew gum: Studies show that chewing gum can help stimulate the part of your brain that remembers information.

Do belly breathing: Oxygen helps relieve stress and increases your ability to think clearly. Breathe in deeply and slowly through your nose as you expand your belly. Then breathe out slowly through your mouth.

Keep a positive attitude: Your attitude can affect how you feel about yourself. Stay positive and tell yourself things like, "I've studied, and I feel confident." Staying positive can help you stay calm and perform your best.

Fact

Standardized testing became common in the United States by World War I (1914–1918). Automatic test scanning machines that read bubble sheets filled out by students were introduced in 1936.

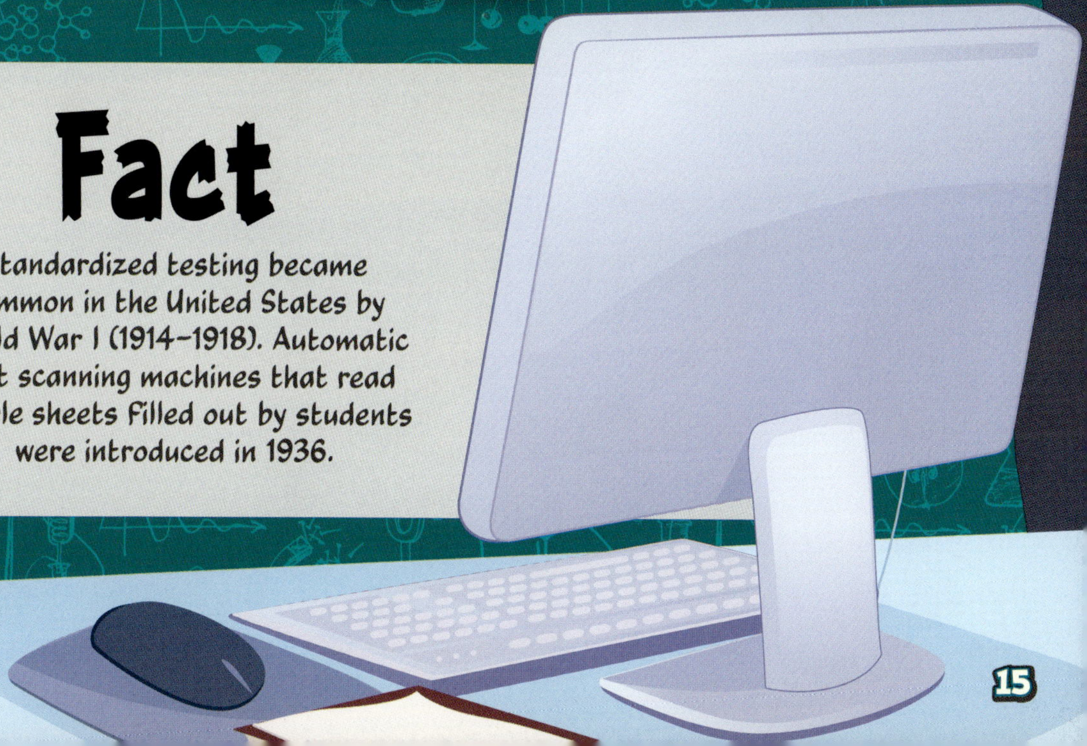

MAKE A STOP-MOTION MOVIE

Quiet on the set! Places, everyone! Lights ... Camera ... Action! Most guys love a fun movie. Whether you like adventure films, funny movies, or science fiction flicks, you can make your own using stop-motion animation. Follow the steps below to make your own blockbuster epic.

STEP 1

WRITE A STORY

Who is your story about? Invent a character and give him or her (or it) a problem to solve. Write it down so you can remember the details. For your first movie, keep it simple.

---

stop-motion—a style of film in which a series of pictures is taken of objects in slightly different positions so they look like they are moving

STEP 2

MAKE A SET AND CHARACTERS

It's time to choose what to use for your characters. You could use clay, paper cutouts, or action figures. Interlocking toys, such as LEGO® bricks, are popular for making stop-motion movies. The toy figures are simple to use, yet have enough detail to make realistic action.

Toy bricks are also handy for making cool sets. Everything stays nicely on the baseplates. You can also use clay, sticks, or rocks to make awesome sets for your story.

STOP-MOTION MASTERS

Stop-motion was one of the first kinds of special effects used to make movies. Willis O'Brien used stop-motion to animate the giant gorilla in the 1933 film *King Kong*. From the 1950s to the 1990s, Ray Harryhausen became famous for his stop-motion work in films such as *Jason and the Argonauts* and *Clash of the Titans*. Harryhausen's work inspired many filmmakers of today. His influence is seen in many modern stop-motion movies such as the *Wallace and Gromit* films, *Paranorman*, and *The LEGO Movie*.

Wallace and Gromit

STEP 3

TAKE THE PHOTOS

You'll need a digital camera or a smartphone. If you have one, a **tripod** is useful for holding the camera steady. Set up your scene with your characters in it. Let's say you're animating a football game. Take a photo of the teams as they are lined up for a passing play. Then move the figures a little as if they are running on the field. Photograph the new positions. Then move the figures a tiny bit again and take another photo. Repeat this process several times until your scene is finished.

TIP: Experiment with a variety of angles, close-ups, and long-range shots. It can create different moods during the scene.

tripod—a stand with three legs; tripods hold cameras steady

STEP 4

ANIMATE

Load your photos onto a computer. Then use a movie-making program, such as iMovie, to put together your film. Load your photos into the computer program and tell it how many frames to use for each photo. A rate of three frames per photo is common.

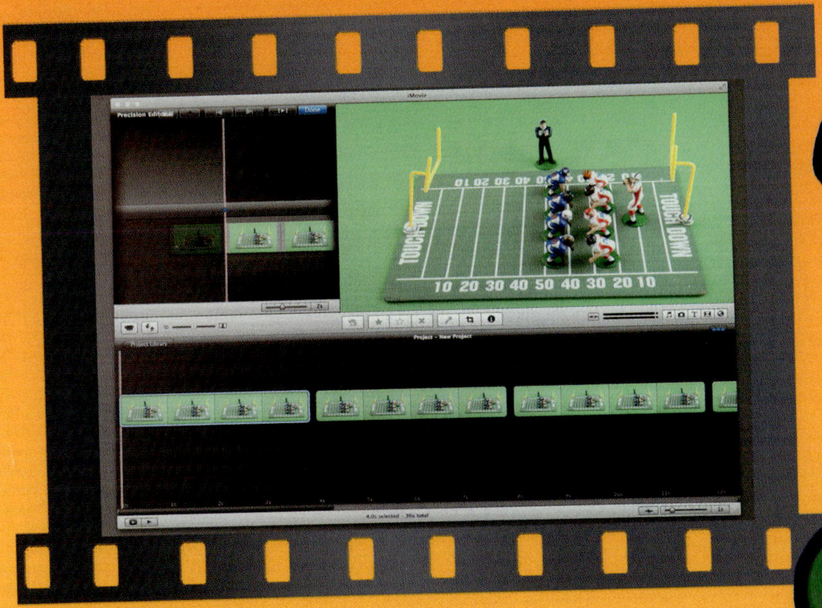

STEP 5

ADD SOUND

If you want music, drag song files into the movie timeline. Or you can use a microphone to record speaking parts for your characters. You can also find free explosions and other sound effects to use in your film online. Once you're ready, click "play" and you'll be watching your very own stop-motion movie!

STEP 6

SHARE IT

You can share your movie with friends by posting it to a blog or on YouTube. As you get more practice, you can write more complicated stories and use different materials to make your movies.

WHO'S MORE AWESOME?

TONY HAWK

THE KID:	became a pro skateboarder by age 14
THE RECORD:	has won more than 70 skateboarding contests
AWESOME INVENTION:	In 1999 Hawk became the first person to pull off the "900." This spine-tingling trick includes two-and-a-half spins in the air from the top of a half-pipe ramp.
AWESOME FACT:	A video game series is based on Hawk's achievements.
AWESOME ADULT:	In his mid-40s, Hawk is still skating and pulling off amazing tricks.
HELPING OTHERS:	The Tony Hawk Foundation raises funds to help build skateboarding parks, especially in low-income neighborhoods.

A lot of guys have achieved amazing things during their lives. However, the guys listed here accomplished more things as young men than many people do in their entire lives. And even as adults, their adventures show that growing up doesn't mean you have to stop being awesome!

RICHARD BRANSON

THE KID:	Branson began a magazine called *Student* at age 16. When he was 22, he founded Virgin Records, one of the most successful record companies of all time.
THE RECORD:	at age 60, became the oldest person to kitesurf across the English Channel
AWESOME INVENTION:	founded the company Virgin Galactic to build spaceships for carrying tourists into space
AWESOME FACT:	crossed both the Atlantic Ocean and Pacific Ocean in a hot air balloon
AWESOME ADULT:	planning to do the first manned dive to the Puerto Rico Trench, the deepest spot in the Atlantic Ocean
HELPING OTHERS:	has given millions of dollars to charities to fight disease and global warming

kitesurf—an extreme sport in which someone rides a surfboard while holding a large sail that captures the wind to pull the rider along

DEAL WITH STICKY SITUATIONS

How to Handle Bullying

If someone is bullying you on the bus, at school, at the local park, or on the Internet, you need to deal with it. It's never OK for someone to make you feel scared or unsafe. Try these ideas to deal with someone who likes to pick on you or others.

IGNORE HIM. Most people bully because they want others to cry, act scared, or get upset. But if you play it cool, many times the bullying will stop.

STAND UP TO HIM. If someone is bullying you, he usually won't expect you to stand up to him. Sometimes just telling him, loud and clear, to knock it off will do the trick. Act brave and strong, even if you don't feel that way.

ESCAPE. If you feel you are in danger, run away as quickly as you can and find an adult.

GET AN ADULT TO HELP. If you tried to stop the bullying, but it didn't work, you need to get help from someone in charge. If you're at school, talk to a teacher, principal, or counselor. Outside of school you can share the problem with a parent or another adult you trust.

How to Resolve a Conflict

IF A COUPLE OF YOUR FRIENDS ARE ARGUING, YOU CAN HELP THEM TO TALK IT OUT. OFFER TO MEDIATE THE CONFLICT. THAT MEANS YOU'LL WORK WITH THEM TO SOLVE THE PROBLEM IN A WAY THAT WORKS FOR EVERYONE. HERE ARE SOME TIPS ON HOW TO HELP RESOLVE AN ARGUMENT.

Let each person talk: Ask the guys to take turns talking about how they feel and what they want. Don't let them interrupt, attack, or accuse each other. This is a time for each person to show respect for the other's feelings.

Summarize the situation: Repeat the problem back to them as you see it. Describe the solutions that each person would like to see.

Brainstorm solutions: Each person should take some time to think about different ways to solve the problem. The solutions need to address what each person wants. Remind your friends that they will probably need to make a compromise.

Agree on a solution: Choose a solution that works best for everyone. It should be something your friends will each mostly like, but will not make them 100 percent happy. That's how compromise works.

Help put the solution into action: Actions speak louder than words. Make an effort to make sure the compromise works. For example, if your friends' argument is about sharing video game time, offer to track the time of each player's turn.

mediate—to work with two people who disagree to find a solution to a problem

compromise—to agree to something that is not exactly what either side wants in order to make a decision

MAKE YOUR ROOM AWESOME

You spend a lot of time in your room. You sleep there. You spend time with friends there. And you probably do your homework there. You may as well make it a cool place to hang out that also reflects your personality. Here are some ideas to help make your room an awesome space. To be safe, get an adult to help you with some of the building projects.

USE VERTICAL SPACE

Give yourself more room by putting up high shelves, hooks, or stacked cubbies where you can store your stuff.

PAINT

Ask a parent if you can paint one or more of your walls a fun color. You could even paint a picture on a wall or get some cool wall stickers.

PUT UP ART

Designate a wall for your awesome photos or posters. Original artwork by you or your friends is unique and totally personal.

USE MOOD LIGHTING

Table lamps create more comfortable lighting than overhead lights. Try using orange or red lightbulbs, or get a lava lamp to give your room a funky look.

SET UP A SPECIAL AREA If you have enough space, set aside part of the room as a workspace. You can use it for doing homework or a hobby such as building models or creating your stop-motion movie.

DECORATE
There are tons of different items you can use to decorate your room. Consider adding a unique wall clock, cool sculptures, or weird plants.

CHANGE THE SURFACE
Try to find a cool rug for the floor or a fun bedspread for your bed.

TURN UP THE TUNES
No room is complete without a few tunes to liven things up. Set up an MP3 player or radio to listen to your favorite music.

KEEP YOUR STUFF PRIVATE

Does your little brother or sister snoop around in your room when you're not there? Your siblings will respect your space if you talk to them maturely. Be clear that you want them to stay out of your stuff. And let them know that you'll respect their space too. Be respectful and you'll earn respect in return. Of course, if necessary, you may need to find a way to keep your things private. Get a file box or a desk that you can keep locked to keep prying eyes away from your stuff.

SPOOK YOUR SIBLING

Is Halloween your favorite holiday? Or maybe you like April Fools' Day. Either way, this harmless trick is a great way to scare the wits out of your kid brother or sister. You can use this sneaky science trick to spook your parents too!

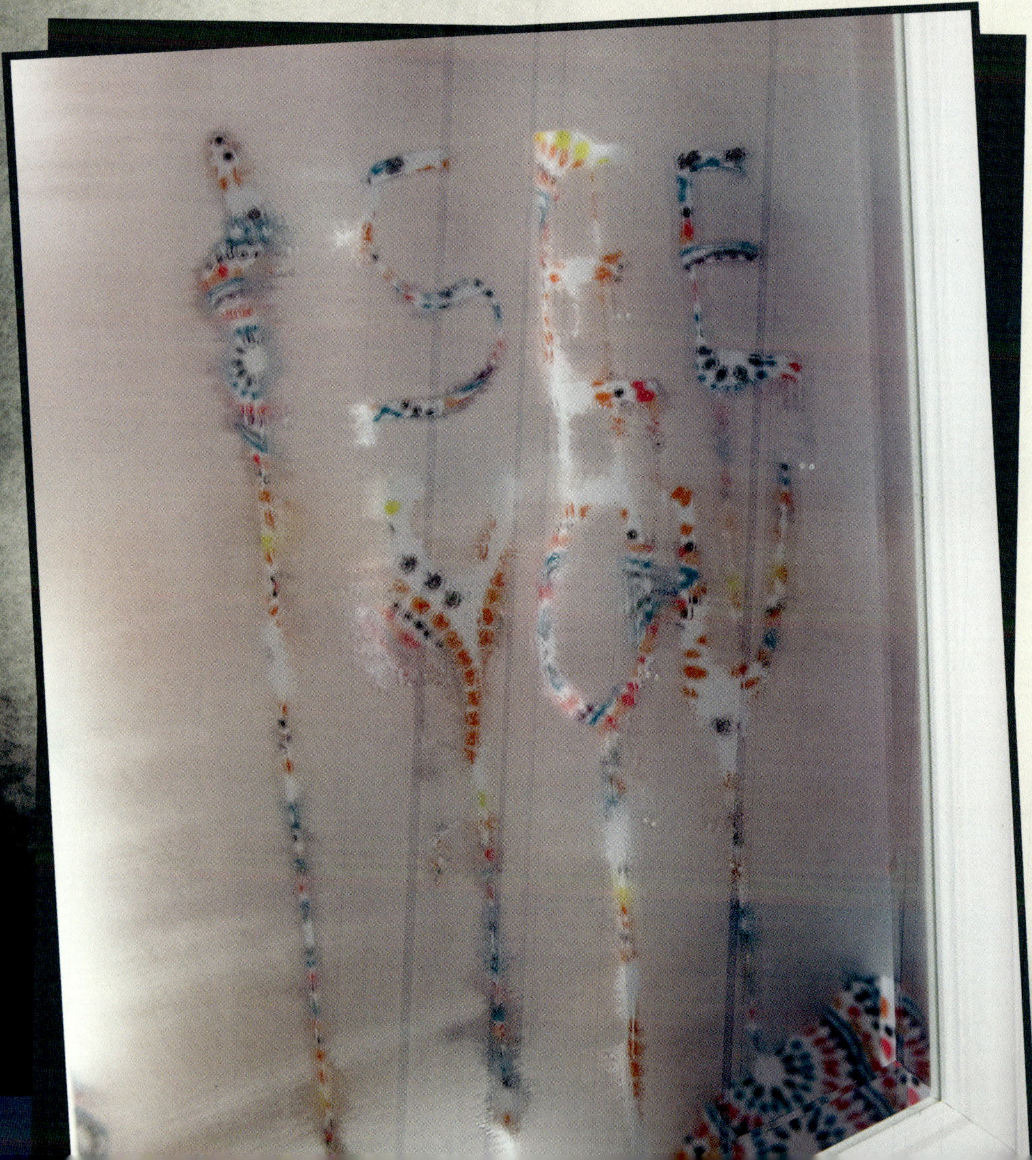

HERE'S WHAT YOU NEED:

- a cotton swab
- a glass of water
- liquid dish soap

Step 1: Mix a few drops of liquid soap into the water so it dissolves.

Step 2: Just before your brother or sister goes to take a hot shower, take the soap solution and cotton swab to the bathroom.

Step 3: Using the cotton swab like a pen, write a haunting or funny message on the bathroom mirror. The words will be invisible on the mirror. Keep dipping your swab in the soap solution to keep it wet.

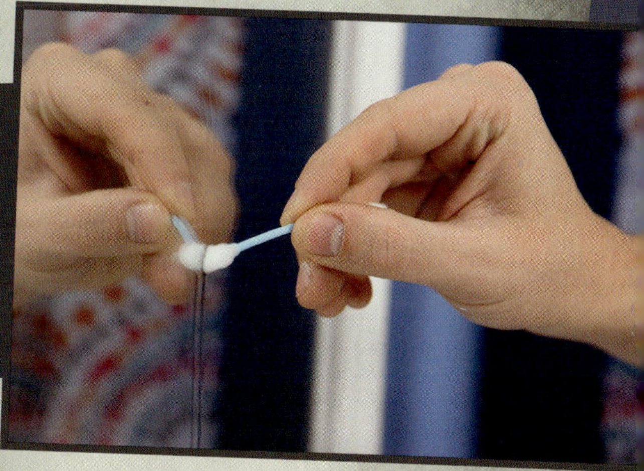

Step 4: Quickly sneak out and get rid of the evidence. Dump out the soap solution and throw away the cotton swabs. Then wait for the fun to start.

Step 5: When your brother or sister gets into the shower, be sure the bathroom door is closed so the steam stays inside. As the mirror fogs up, your secret message will appear on it. When your victim gets out of the shower, he or she will see your spooky message!

KEEP YOUR BIKE IN TIP-TOP SHAPE

Your bike is important! It's probably one of the most expensive things you own. It may also be the only transportation you can use without an adult. You need to take good care of it. Follow these tips to help keep your bike in great shape.

KEEP IT DRY Store your bike indoors so it's not exposed to the weather. Moisture can cause rust and ruin any moving parts. If you can't store it inside, get a tarp to cover it. After riding in the rain, be sure to wipe down your bike to dry it.

KEEP IT CLEAN You don't need to use soap, which can cause rust. But wipe down your bike with a damp cloth when it's dirty. If it's covered in mud, spray it down with a hose first. Pay special attention to moving parts, especially the chain. Sand and dirt can ruin it. Use a stiff brush to clean the grime off of the chain. Don't forget to dry off your bike after cleaning it.

LUBRICATE THE CHAIN Use a special bicycle lubricant, being careful to cover every inch of the chain. Hold a cloth under the chain as you apply the lubricant. This will keep the slick stuff off the ground and your brakes, which could prevent them from working well. Do this about once a week if you're a regular rider.

KEEP THE TIRES FIRM Check your tire pressure before every ride. The proper pressure is often found on the sidewall of the tires. But most tires need pressure of about 75 pounds per square inch. Use a pressure gauge if you have one. Otherwise, you can pump up the tires until they feel nice and hard.

WATCH THE BRAKES Check your brake pads every month or so to be sure they're not too worn down. If they're getting thin, it's time to replace them. Also be sure they contact the rim of the wheels and not the tires.

If you can squeeze the brake lever all the way down, you need to tighten the cable. Squeeze the brake calipers together to release the cable. Then use an Allen wrench or bike tool to loosen the nut on the brake caliper. Pull about 1/8 inch (0.32 centimeter) of cable through. Then tighten the nut and reattach the cable. Test the brake lever to see how the brakes respond. If they still feel loose, repeat the process as needed until they work correctly.

---

lubricant—a slippery substance used to allow the surfaces of two objects to easily slide over each other

GLOSSARY

Allies (AL-eyz)—a group of countries that fought together in World War II including the United States, England, France, the Soviet Union, and others

cipher (SY-fur)—a code that uses letters or symbols to represent letters of the alphabet

compromise (KAHM-pruh-myz)—to agree to something that is not exactly what either side wants in order to make a decision

hydrate (HYE-drayt)—to achieve a healthy balance of fluids in the body

intelligence (in-TEL-uh-jenss)—the ability to learn and understand information

kitesurf (KITE-surf)—an extreme sport in which someone rides a surfboard while holding a large sail that captures the wind to pull the rider along

lubricant (LOOB-rih-kuhnt)—a slippery substance used to allow the surfaces of two objects to easily slide over each other

mediate (MEE-dee-ayt)—to work with two people who disagree to find a solution to a problem

special effect (SPESH-uhl uh-FEKT)—an illusion created for movies or TV using special props, camera systems, computer graphics, and other methods

stop-motion (STOP MO-shun)—a style of filmmaking in which a series of pictures is taken of objects in slightly different positions so they look like they are moving

tripod (TRYE-pod)—a stand with three legs; tripods hold cameras steady

READ MORE

Bell-Rehwoldt, Sheri. *The Kids' Guide to Duct Tape Projects.* Kids' Guides. North Mankato, Minn.: Capstone Press, 2012.

Enz, Tammy. *Zoom It: Invent New Machines that Move.* Invent It. North Mankato, Minn.: Capstone Press, 2012.

Gill, Mickey and Cheryl Gill. *Dude Diary 3.0: Write Stuff, Draw Random Things, Destroy if Needed.* Longwood, Fla.: Fine Print Publishing Company, 2012.

INTERNET SITES

FactHound offers a safe, fun way to find Internet sites related to this book. All of the sites on FactHound have been researched by our staff.

Here's all you do:

Visit *www.facthound.com*

Type in this code: 9781476539249

WWW.FACTHOUND.COM®

Super-cool stuff!

Check out projects, games and lots more at
www.capstonekids.com

INDEX